T0207784

MY TWO HIGH SCHOOLS, WICOMICO and ANNAPOLIS

A Memoir

JACK SHILKRET

MY TWO HIGH SCHOOLS, WICOMICO AND ANNAPOLIS
A MEMOIR

Copyright © 2022 Jack Shilkret.

All rights reserved. No part of this book may be used or reproduced by any means, graphic, electronic, or mechanical, including photocopying, recording, taping or by any information storage retrieval system without the written permission of the author except in the case of brief quotations embodied in critical articles and reviews.

iUniverse books may be ordered through booksellers or by contacting:

iUniverse
1663 Liberty Drive
Bloomington, IN 47403
www.iuniverse.com
844-349-9409

Because of the dynamic nature of the Internet, any web addresses or links contained in this book may have changed since publication and may no longer be valid. The views expressed in this work are solely those of the author and do not necessarily reflect the views of the publisher, and the publisher hereby disclaims any responsibility for them.

Any people depicted in stock imagery provided by Getty Images are models, and such images are being used for illustrative purposes only.
Certain stock imagery © Getty Images.

ISBN: 978-1-6632-3360-8 (sc)
ISBN: 978-1-6632-3342-4 (e)

Library of Congress Control Number: 2022901810

Print information available on the last page.

iUniverse rev. date: 01/28/2022

I see it as ironic that I had two high schools in my life, while my father never finished high school. My father was a Russian immigrant who left his strict uncle's home when he was sixteen and never went back to school. My first high school was in Salisbury, Maryland, a small town where my father owned and operated a well-known lady's shoe store. I went to Wicomico High School, which I will refer to as Wi Hi. It was the only public high school for white students in the still segregated town. It was a strict place.

"Did you just slam that door? Go back and close it right!" Our vice principal was yelling at my friend, Harry. He did what he was told as I stood there, a bit frightened. We called our teachers Mr. and Ms. and mostly did what we were told. I did have some teachers who were respected for the most part. However, there were times when they were really disrespected. I never disrespected a teacher at Wi Hi. Also, I never thought during my years at Wi Hi that I would become a teacher myself.

Ms. White was my geometry teacher. She always started every class with some sort of declarative sentence, such as, "*I love geometry!*" I just sat there and mostly listened and tried to solve the problems she put on the chalkboard. I did not always succeed.

Ms. White ran her class on a schedule set to a desk clock to which she frequently referred. One morning she was not in the room when I got to class, and four students were at the front of the room, examining the objects on her desk. One of the students, Bill, knocked her desk clock on the floor and put it back just before she entered the room as the students were hurrying back to their desks. It did not take her long before she noticed that her clock was broken. She struggled through the class anyway. At the end of the class that day she stated very firmly that she expected the student who had broken her clock to stay after class and confess. The bell rang for class change, and I left quickly.

The next day when I returned to geometry class, I noticed a new clock on her desk, and she was still thinking about the broken clock. After talking about her clock during class, she asked us to take out a piece of paper and write down the name of the student who broke her clock before we left. I did not write anything on my paper, but some of my classmates did. The next day she was quite mad at us. She told us that some of us had disrespected her by writing false names on their sheet of paper. Mickey Mantle, Ms. White, and Mr. Nobody were just some of names she read to us. She never discovered who broke her clock.

Another teacher I remember well was Mr. Howard. He was the father of one of my friends at Wi Hi, John. In his gruff voice, he occasionally told us stories in class that had nothing to do with chemistry. One of the stories he told was about a school baseball game with Crisfield that had occurred decades ago. In a close game, one of the players on Wi Hi's team got to third base. A shoreman from Crisfield appeared on the field near the base with a stern expression on his face, holding a shotgun. His whole demeanor meant *you better stay right where you are!*

Of course, we had lab in chemistry class. Mr. Howard would frequently say, "If you copy the lab problems, make sure you copy from someone who got the problems right." I would smile to myself whenever he said that, because I occasionally copied the problems from his son's lab book. I never understood chemistry, but I liked Mr. Howard.

There were other teachers that I remember a bit less vividly. One was Ms. Mesick, my French teacher, who did not speak with a French accent. She would sometimes jokingly allude to her "cousin" Lenny Moore, a well-known Black pro football player on the Baltimore Colts. I never saw much humor in that.

Then there was my Latin teacher, Ms. Hanks. I remember her mostly for getting sick and being unable to finish the year. The school got a substitute to finish the year for her, and somehow, we talked her into letting us play Scrabble in Latin in class. The Latin part quickly got dropped, and we finished the year playing Scrabble in English in Latin class.

I also remember Ms. Tanner, my English teacher. Today I would describe her as histrionic, but then I just thought she was weird. She would attempt to act out the subject of the day by marching up and down the aisles, sometimes reciting the words from a poem or a play. It was an unusual combination of marching and dancing, very strange. She would also frequently complain about beer cans and other trash that she saw by the side of the road. There was a rumor that I remember that a group of classmates, as a cruel prank, had littered her yard with beer and soda cans.

I also recall my psychology teacher, Mr. Hope. He had an appropriate name, and I remember him fondly. I never suspected how soon I would become a psychology teacher myself. He was also a minister, and some of his classes did have a sermon like quality to them.

Then there was my band teacher, Mr. Dwyer. I had learned to play the clarinet in junior high under the direction of my band teacher, Mr. Pressman. Now, after being demoted from first clarinet, Mr. Dwyer was asking me if there was anything he could do for me, probably seeing that I was very bored in his band class. "Teach me to play the piano," I said. He did try, but I did not have a piano at home, and I never really worked at it. This was the only time that a high school teacher asked how he could help me.

Band did become an important part of my high school life, starting in junior high, where we had permission to make a lot of noise and take part in parades. What kid would not like that? However, my clarinet experience did take a sort of backward direction. By eighth grade we had learned our instruments well enough to form a band, and we practiced at least three time a week. We also learned to march for parades and later for football games. My father even led an effort to get us uniforms, which we wore with pride.

Now to my clarinet experience. In either eighth or ninth grade, I was chosen to be the solo clarinetist. I did not really play that well; my technique and rhythm were lacking. But I did have a good tone, and I guess that is why I was chosen. But then Mr. Pressman introduced us to the challenge method. He declared that if anyone wanted to challenge a soloist for his position, he would officiate the challenge, and the winner would get the position. It did not take awfully long for my friend Franz to challenge me. There were at least three challenges between us. Franz ended up as the soloist, a position he kept all through high school. He eventually went to a prestigious music school in Baltimore and later became a band director himself.

My progression with the clarinet was in the other direction: down, down and down. I went down to second clarinet music in my first year of high school, and as a senior all the way down to the simple music of third clarinet. In high school, my younger brother Bob was challenging Franz for the soloist position. That was one of the few things in high school that Bob did not attain. I was only glad to be in the band with my friends and knew that after high school my clarinet experience would be over.

To better understand my first high school experience, one can look at the class "will" that was published with the yearbook. For me they printed, "Jack Shilkret leaves running." As I think back, I know this was certainly true. From the end of junior high, I began fantasizing about what I would do when I left Salisbury and went on to college. I had no idea where I would go to college or what I would do, but really did want to leave my hometown.

However, my life in Salisbury was rather good. My family life was certainly privileged. I lived in a white stucco home that was striking, located on a main street of the town. It was a bit small for our family of four or five, with one and a half baths, but was adequate. My father operated his store every day from 9–5 or to 9:30 on Fridays. My mother played mahjong or cards, went antiquing, or found other ways to pass time. Our family had a maid who did all the housework and prepared all the meals from Monday to Friday. This did not seem special or unusual to me, since all our parents' friends also had help. When I was younger, and later when my mother had a serious medical issue, we also had a nanny, Margaret, who later became a close family friend.

I have a brother, Bob, who is one year younger than me. As children, my mother always dressed us alike, like twins; but as we got older that stopped. I was called J.P. as a child, mainly to distinguish me from the daughter, Jackie, of my parents' best friends. In early childhood, Bobby and J.P. were always together. Eventually my father remodeled the attic into two rooms, and even though the steps to the rooms were very steep, Bob moved upstairs and took over one of the rooms. I always saw this as his declaration of independence.

Bobby and J.P. 1947

In elementary school, Bob and I were in separate grades but still together much of the time. We both did very well in elementary school, but in junior high Bob began to distinguish himself from me and most of the other students too. I was a good student in junior high and got A's and B's. Bob got all A's, and this continued into high school too. Since I was older, I did get my driver's license first and quickly was assigned the job of taking our maid home after dinner. Later, Bob and I carefully planned a trip to Langley Park, Maryland. We visited our cousins Milton, Judy, and their children Steve, Gene, and Tina. We really enjoyed being with them, and the suburban area was a nice change from Salisbury. My cousin Steve, was interested in music and was a member of his high school band like us. I was a bit envious of him, because he went to a larger high school and seemed to be happier than I was at Wi Hi.

In high school Bob played clarinet too, and band was one of the activities we shared. The other was a duck-pin bowling team that we organized and entered in a men's league on Friday nights. One day after school, I noticed our current maid, Elsie was acting strange. She seemed different and uninvolved. Then, somehow, I knew she was intoxicated. At first, I did not know what to do. I did not drink alcohol while in Wi Hi, and neither did Bob. I checked the Shabbos wine, and it was mostly gone. I went to Elsie and told her it was time to take her home. I guess Bob and I made our own dinner that night.

In junior high school and high school, Bob and I had our own friends. Bob continued to get all A's and was a superior student. I was never resentful of Bob's success, partly because our parents never compared us and treated us the same no matter what. That was an unspoken rule with them. My interest in girls developed somewhat slowly, but after I learned to drive and was able to use one of our two cars, I became what might be called a serial dater. It took me weeks to get up the nerve to call up a girl and ask her out. If she agreed, I would pick her up at her home, meet her parents, and then take her to a movie. I was too nervous to form much of a relationship with any one girl and never had a real girlfriend in high school. I had very few second dates. I must have dated seven or eight girls while in high school, but few more than once. When my senior prom came up, I wanted to go but did not know who to go with. I ended up asking the younger daughter of one of my parents' friends. Of course, it ended up being a family affair, with movies being taken at both homes. It was awkward because I had never dated her before. What really surprised me is that after the prom, we went to a party at the home of one of my friends, but Judy, my date, seemed to know my classmates better than I did.

Jack's high school home

A turning point might have been on a Sunday afternoon when Bob and I had been asked by our Dad to rake the leaves. When he came home from his Sunday golf, he was not satisfied with our raking; we may not have done any at all. Dad did have a temper. He yelled at us and insisted that we go to the store with him. When we got there, he had us go the stock room, and he had us stand there while he moved the shoe boxes all around, shifting stock. "I will show you what work really is," he said. He probably lectured us for twenty minutes or more, shifting stock the whole time. Dad never knew how that incident encouraged my growing independence. I thought to myself then that I was not going to take over the store, and I certainly knew by then that Bob never would either. I knew that I wanted to leave Salisbury when I went to college and lead an independent life, but I had no idea, no real plans how that would happen. My parents always supported Bob and me in choosing our own way, and I knew I would have the chance in the future. I just did not know what that choice would be.

After I graduated Wi Hi in 1960, I decided to attend the University of Maryland and major in psychology. I had applied to four colleges but was only accepted by two. I had already seen the University of Maryland, so my mother went with me to Philadelphia for a college visit. When I realized that Temple was a city college without a campus I quickly decided on Maryland. That summer before college, I was able to get a job as a counselor at Pine Forest Camp, where my parents had sent us for five years. I enjoyed being outside and teaching ten-year-olds how to play sports. It helped get me ready for being away from home when I went to college.

Jack's high school graduation

In the fall of 1960, my parents drove me to the University of Maryland and helped me find my dormitory room. In those days there was a dormitory shortage, and on-campus dormitory rooms were only assigned to students from the state of Maryland. The out-of-state students not only paid more tuition but also had to find a room off campus or join a fraternity or sorority. When we found my room, it was on the third floor of Washington Hall, an exceptionally large room with at least six beds. I had been assigned to a room with five other men. I was a bit puzzled at first, but I quickly discovered that all my new roommates were Jewish like me. I had wanted to have Jewish friends like my parents did, but soon discovered that in college it is not good to have too many roommates.

I do not know whether the dorm officials who assigned us this room thought we would like to be with other men of the Jewish faith or not. They should have realized that all freshmen would do better in their own room with one other person, so now I see the situation as discriminatory. While sharing a room with five other men was amusing for a week or so, it soon got old. For the next two years, as I was discovering what college was like, I was also involved in a series of room changes until I was satisfied with my living situation.

The person who decided to assign six Jewish men to a single room obviously did not know that Jewish men can be just as diverse as any group of six. One of my roommates was an Orthodox Jew and would get up every morning at six and put on tefillin and pray. Another came back from fraternity rush without his shoes, commenting that he did not remember if he took his date back to her dormitory. I made a few friends, but quickly realized that my evenings needed to be spent in the library.

Since I had not had time to make friends, in the first months of college I got involved with a series of room changes until I was satisfied with my living situation. Among the rejected roommates was a man who would light up a cigarette every morning before his feet touched the ground. Another had been placed on disciplinary probation and thought he was entitled to a single room. When he started talking to me about going into professors' offices and stealing their tests, he got his wish for a single room.

Time went by quickly the first year, and the work was challenging. I had to study hard to maintain a C+ average. Later, as community college professor, I would tell my students that when I went to Maryland it was easy to get in but hard to stay; now it is hard to get in but easy to stay. Some of my first friends at Maryland either flunked out or left before graduating. Time passed; I finally got a pretty girl friend—Ruthie! When I expressed some confusion about the future, she advised me to change majors to education and study to become a teacher like she was doing. So, in my junior year I transferred to secondary education and started studying to become a high school teacher. I had already become a more serious student and started working part time at a nearby department store selling ladies' shoes. Ruthie and I ended up getting married in the spring.

As I was finishing my senior year, I was taking all education courses and vaguely knew what I was going to do after graduation. I did not know whether I would teach in a senior high or a junior high or whether I could get a teaching job at all, since mine was an extremely popular major. That January I applied to at least four Maryland public school systems for a teaching job. I got one request for an interview. So, in the spring of 1964 I drove for my first and only interview for a public school job to Annapolis, Maryland. I was just finishing my student-teaching assignment at a nearby high school. My student-teaching assignment had been as a U.S. history teacher, and my only real teaching was three-week preparation on the presidency of Theodore Roosevelt, which I had taught by myself for about a week and a half. So, when Ruthie and I drove to Annapolis, I had not done much teaching and had no idea what to expect.

I found Annapolis High School in the middle of town. There was a sprawling three-story building with a football field behind it and a smaller, brick building with an outside staircase leading to the second floor. As I looked over Annapolis High School for the first time, I had a memory of a rainy night five or six years ago when I went there as a member of the Wi Hi band. Ruthie waited in the car as I climbed up the steps to my future. Annapolis Senior High School was to become my second-high school. I did not know it then, but I was to learn more during this four-year experience than I had in the previous four at college or the four at Wi Hi.

I was greeted as I entered the school by the vice principal, Mr. Will. He introduced himself and led me to a nearby conference room, where he introduced me to the principal, Mr. Flack, and another man, Mr. Dean. Mr. Flack did most of the talking. He was friendly and to the point. I do not think Mr. Will spoke at all. Mr. Dean seemed solemn as he spoke. The principle asked me how many psychology courses I had taken in Maryland. I replied five, fearing it would not be enough. Then I heard that Mr. Dean was the school's main psychology teacher and that he had only taken one psychology course. Then Mr. Flack asked me if I had taken a geography course. Yes, I replied. "Introduction to Geography" was required in my major. I had taken it a year ago, but had to repeat last spring because it was one of the two classes in which I had received a D. I repeated it with the same professor and struggled through with a C. Fortunately, I didn't have my transcript with me and do not think it had been sent. Mr. Flack smiled as he looked at me and asked, "Would you like to teach for us next year? Four classes of psychology and one of geography." I smiled and said that would be fine. I was hired on the spot, just as I realized that I would be taking some, if not all, of Mr. Dean's classes. Mr. Flack said that psychology was very popular at the school and that next year I would probably be able to teach all psychology. My first-year salary would be $4,500. I was excited as I left the room and walked down the steps to tell Ruthie the good news. The whole interview lasted less than a half hour.

As I drove back to our apartment in Hyattsville, I realized that the future was now. I had had some close calls later with my college advisor about getting my degree. He did not know if I had taken enough classes, but I convinced him that I had. I did not attend my graduation. I did not like big crowds and thought it would be boring. Little did I know that later I would attend many graduations as a job requirement as a community college professor. They certainly were boring! I never did attend a graduation ceremony for any of the three college degrees that I earned.

I kept my job at the department store for the summer and worked on plans for the first year of teaching psychology and geography. I put most of my outlines on large index cards. The summer of 1964 went by quickly as we made plans for our new apartment in Annapolis. However, we did take at least one trip to Salisbury and Ocean City, Maryland.

We drove the thirty-mile trip to Ocean City from my home in Salisbury. In 1964, Ocean City had not developed much, and there was nothing but a six-lane highway and empty beach from 14th street to the Delaware state line. However, there was a brand-new hotel, the Carousel, that was being built by a friend of President Johnson toward the end of Ocean City. That was the beach where we planned to swim. My mother and father set up our chairs on the beach, and Bob and Ruthie went on ahead to the ocean. I stopped to rent a raft, something I always did, because a trip to the beach had to involve "riding the waves." I got the raft and headed toward the ocean.

I ran into the ocean and looked for Ruthie and Bob. It took me a few seconds to realize that they were both about fifty yards ahead of me and struggling to stay afloat in the waves. For a few seconds, I thought I might have to save them both, but then I saw that Bob was breaking through the waves and seemed ok. Ruthie was still having trouble. I did not realize that she had never swam in the ocean before. I paddled the raft out to her, got her up on the raft sideways, and then pulled it across the ocean until I could start angling it toward shore. When we reached the shore, she was a bit frightened but ok. I do not remember if there was much drama made about my rescue. I do not think that Ruthie went back into the ocean, but I know I did. One of my father's friends took a memorable picture of us to mark the occasion.

Ocean City, Maryland 1964; my family

In early summer, I took Ruthie and my cousins to the downtown Washington branch of my department store to buy our furniture, and they could buy whatever they wanted using my twelve and a half percent discount. We bought our bedroom furniture: a bed, two large chests of drawers, and a desk. My cousins bought mostly clothes. It was an exciting day! In August we had a moving company move us to Annapolis, where we had rented a brand new apartment about half a mile from Annapolis High School. We soon had a baby girl, Robin, and spent most of our time together learning how to take care of her.

I do not remember my first class at Annapolis, but I am sure it went well. The other teachers were mostly helpful and friendly. I was given a classroom in the large three-story building on the third floor. I discovered that I would get an hour break every day and a half hour for lunch. I guess I could have taken my breaks in the classroom, but I discovered that the building had two teachers' break rooms, one for men and one for women. I never went into the women's teachers' break room, although some of the men did to talk to the women. So, I found myself downstairs in the men's teachers break room every day.

It was sort of funny. There we were, at least eight men teachers, looking at each other, making small talk, and wondering what we should do. I do not think we even thought about checking papers or preparing lessons. We decided to play cards. At first, we may have considered gambling for money, but must have known right away that was not a good idea. We decided to play Hearts. We all seemed to know how to play the game. That is what I did during my breaks for the four years I was at Annapolis High School. For at least two years, some of us had our lunch break either before or after our class breaks, so we would play cards for an hour and a half. We would even yell out "second shift" when some of the players changed.

Our principal, Mr. Flack, would sometimes come down to the teachers' lounge. We would say hello, and he would usually say, "You're playing cards," in a friendly way.

Someone would invariably reply, "Yes, we are playing Hearts, would you like to play?" He then would say no and hurry back up the steps.

I did have one very frightening experience in the men's break room, and it occurred in either the first or second day that I was teaching at Annapolis High School. We had not organized the card game yet, and we were standing around talking. One of the other teachers, Reggie, was talking to me, and our conversation turned angry. Reggie did not like my tone or my words. I continued the argument, even though I did not know Reggie very well. Suddenly Reggie grabbed me by the shoulders and threw me to the floor. I knew I was not going to fight him, but I was shocked and angry. I pulled myself up, gave Reggie an angry look, and left. I realized that at least five men had witnessed the incident. I wandered around the school for ten minutes considering my options. I could report him to the administration, or I could go back to the break room. I went back to my classroom.

The next day I do not think Reggie was in the break room. I vaguely remember him apologizing to me, but I am not sure of that. I do not think that Reggie ever joined the card game. I ignored him from then on whenever I saw him. I ran into him many years later, and we talked briefly, but not about the incident. I have seen him a few other times, and our conversations have been friendly. During my first year at Annapolis High, I decided I did not want to be a high school teacher all my life. I remember a student, Janice, talking to me. She said, "My grandmother and my mother had Ms. Davis as their English teacher. Do you think you will teach my grandchildren?" I replied, "I sure hope not." She seemed a bit surprised by my honesty. I thought that maybe I could teach at a community college or a college. But to do that I would need at least a master's degree. I knew that I needed to qualify for the University of Maryland if I wanted to work for my advanced degree there, and I discovered that George Washington University was offering a course, "Industrial Psychology," at the Naval Academy. I checked with someone at Maryland to be sure the class would qualify me for graduate school. I figured I needed an A or B to qualify.

I went to the Naval Academy and found my class, I sat in the middle of the room. A man who looked like a Naval Officer in uniform was sitting smiling at us in the front of the room. Other men came into the room and filled the desks until there were about twenty men in the room. There were no women. The Naval Officer stood up and introduced himself. "I am Captain Brunt. This is our textbook, *Industrial Psychology.*" Most of us students had a copy of the text, having previously purchased it at the

Academy bookstore. He held up the book above his head and quickly lowered it to look at it. He was looking at the table of contents. "Welcome to class," said Captain Brunt. "Who would like to lead the first chapter, 'Introduction'?" Someone raised his hand. The captain shook his head and jotted something in a note pad. "Who would like to lead the second chapter, 'Industrial Structures?'" Again, someone raised his hand, and the captain asked for his name and jotted it down in the note pad. "Who would like to lead the third chapter, 'Personnel?'" I thought I better figure out which one I wanted to do; this guy is going to get us to do his job. At the right time I found a chapter, "Personality," and volunteered for it. Once class began, it went smoothly but was boring. I do not recall any tests or written assignments. There was a final exam, but that was all. I got an A; I was on my way to graduate school.

You may be getting the idea that teaching then was easier than it is now. You are right. The teachers at Annapolis High School were allowed to do their own thing mostly the way they wanted. I caught on extremely fast. During my four years at Annapolis, I was always treated with respect by the administration, even kindly at times. I made some close friends who really liked me. My years at the school were mostly happy and humorous, but at the time they were more serious incidents. I really did become a skilled teacher.

Recently I attended a reunion of the Annapolis High School Class of 1969. One of my students had become a lawyer. He introduced me and was very complimentary. He even remembered that I had purchased several copies of a book on social psychology and distributed them to class members so they could do exercises and attempt to work at a college level. One thing I did not like were teachers' meetings—those times when we discussed school policy and discipline. The meetings were often boring and seemed to accomplish little. The only one I remember well was discussing whether students would be allowed to wear jeans to class. It took quite a while to decide that they could wear white jeans but not blue or black jeans. I do not think our conclusion was honored by students for awfully long.

Toward the end of my first year, I was told that the supervisor of social studies for the county wanted to evaluate my teaching and that she would be accompanied by the school's supervisor of social studies, Mr. Orr. Since she did not know psychology very well, she wanted to observe my geography class. I agreed without comment.

I was teaching geography by reading the chapter in the book and then presenting it to the class. The class was non-academic, what was called "general" in those days. I had learned to get along with the class very well, and they all seemed to enjoy my instruction and liked me.

So, the day before the observation, I told the class that we were going to be evaluated by some important officials, and since I wanted them to make a good impression we would "practice" the class today. Then I would teach the exact class again the next day, when we would be observed. I told them not to reveal the plan, and that was a way that all teachers did their best work. Most of them knew what was going on and went along with my plan.

The class was on the geography of Egypt. It started off smoothly, and even though this was my first observation, I was not nervous with the two observers in the back of the room. Halfway through the class, I asked a key question. "As you know, Egypt is an extremely hot, dry country, but it does have a large river, the Nile, to water the crops. How do they get the water to the crops?" No one raised their hand to answer. I asked the question a second time, but no one raised their hand even though I had asked the same question yesterday. Then Barry, a popular and friendly student, raised his hand. Ok, I thought, as I nodded for him to answer. "Buckets," he replied. I smiled, not breaking stride, and explained how they dug canals all along the river to get water to the fields to enable a harvest.

At the end of the class, I went to the back of the room. The supervisors liked the class! They thought the "buckets" answer was hilarious too. That was my only teaching evaluation at Annapolis High School. Later, the supervisor of social studies became a colleague when I became a community college instructor.

The years I taught at Annapolis High School turned out to be historically important, because they were the years that Anne Arundel County public schools were integrated. In school year 1964 the school was completely segregated, and the African American students went to Bates High, less than a quarter of a mile from Annapolis High. I do not recall much mention of future integration during the school year. Toward the end of the year, we were told that next year we would be using the "freedom of choice" option, in which African American students could choose to attend Annapolis High if they wished. When the fall of 1965 arrived, less than fifteen percent of my students were African American. There was no controversy—it just happened. I got along very well with all the students and did not think much about it.

Then, in September of 1966, Bates High School was closed, and all students went to Annapolis. Maybe partly because of integration and certainly because of the turmoil of the times, the school became a bit disrupted, and it was more difficult to teach. I began to have more difficulty with a few white students. I looked a bit like the TV actor Tim Conway, and they began to call me "Ensign Parker," the character he played in a popular comedy show. They would yell the name out in the halls and write it on the chalkboard when I was out of the room. They sometimes drew pictures and left them around the room. I disciplined them by assigning detention, but they did not always serve it. I mostly ignored them and tried to overlook their disrespect and teach my classes.

After my first year at Annapolis High, my relationships with some of the other teachers became deeper. I guess our continual togetherness playing cards contributed; however, my two best friends never joined the card game. I became particularly close to Tom Getz, who was hired to teach five psychology classes with me. I was also friendly with a math teacher, Bo Pauli, and a shop teacher, John Penti. Later I became close friends with John Witti, who was also my neighbor. There were many others.

From the beginning, my close friend and mentor was a biology teacher, Harry Earle, who also had taught psychology. He lived in another section of Annapolis, about three miles away. Our families became so close that at times we would take our daughter Robin and visit them unannounced. Harry taught me how to fill out the attendance book and other expectations and technical matters. He was a dedicated and serious teacher and a great role model for me.

During the last two years at Annapolis, Tom Getz taught in a room right next to mine on the first floor of the old building that later became a community center, Annapolis Hall. We started to cooperate with each other to make teaching easier. By this time, we were both good teachers but wanted to enjoy our work and had a sense of humor about our daily activities as teachers. I was always looking for ways to make my classes interesting and even fun for my students and me.

I discovered that there was a nearby film library at the Naval Academy that had appropriate films for psychology. I made visits there during school time to borrow and return films. I taught a few of my students to operate the film projector so I could be free to do other things. Sometimes Tom and I were able to use a larger room to show the films so that one of us could take longer breaks. If we had a particularly good film, we would show it to the large audience twice, especially at student request. We would sometime say, "Repetition builds retention."

One day Tom talked to me before classes had begun. He was genuinely concerned, because an exceedingly difficult student had been transferred to his favorite class. He said, "Dean was sitting in the school guidance office because the counselors did not know what to do with him." Tom continued, "He is now disturbing my best class. He makes noises like he is driving a truck and does not stop when asked. This is my best class, and he is ruining it. Jack, you have a bad class fourth period. Could you take him into your class?" I agreed. Tom was my friend and I did have a difficult class at that time; my class was a more appropriate placement for Dean. We may have filled out paperwork, I am not sure how we did it, but the next day Dean was in my fourth-period class. For the next few days, Dean did ok and the class went on in its usual matter.

There was a student in that class, George, who had an unusual pattern of behavior. He would be unruly for the first five minutes of class, then he would tire and rest his head on his desk and fall asleep. I would usually let him sleep so I could teach the class. Then he would wake up in the last few minutes of the class and sometimes cause a disturbance. I was teaching in a room that we formerly used for biology. There were all kinds of biology equipment in the back of the room. I noticed Dean looking at some of this equipment. I told him to take his seat, but I did not see that he had taken a pointer that was like a dart. George awoke from his nap and started talking to his classmates. Next, George was wadding up a piece of paper and throwing it right at Dean. Before I could say anything, Dean was hit in the back of his head by the piece of paper. Dean turned around, saw George laughing at him, and he threw the pointer at George. It did not hit him but whizzed by his head just as the bell to end the class rang. I saw Dean moving quickly out of the class with an angry George in pursuit. I was glad to see them go. Dean continued in the class for a few more days, and then he stopped attending school. Later I heard a rumor that he had left his home and was hiding out in a tent in a south Annapolis park.

Another incident later in the year showed how the school administration respected teachers and why we got along so well. One morning, I was teaching my first class, and I heard a knocking on my door. Through the window I saw that Mr. Orr, our supervisor of social studies, had come over from the other building to see me. When I opened the door, Mr. Orr spoke, "Mr. Shilkret did you know there was a fight between two girls yesterday in your fourth period class?" He named the girls. I was quite surprised, but quickly figured out what had happened.

I replied, "No, I was out of the class for a few minutes or so."

"Well, there was!" Mr. Orr said. "There was a big fight that was disturbing to the other students in the class, and I have heard they might be a problem with the girls today; that's why I came over, to warn you."

"Thank you for telling me, Mr. Orr," I replied. He left without another word.

I quickly understood what had happened. In the fourth period class, I had a student operating the projector while I left the room for about ten minutes. When I came back, I saw that the projector was still running, and the film was winding round and round on the take-up reel. "Oh, Harry must have neglected to turn off the projector," I thought. I turned off the projector and rewound the film. Later a student told me that the fight between the two girls was quite disturbing. Some students had to get out of the way as they wrestled with one another. As soon as the bell rang for lunch, everyone quickly left the room. The next day the girls were back in class. I told them not to fight again. I do not recall any punishment for them.

By early March 1968, I was in my last class for the Master of Education degree at the University of Maryland and had applied for a job as an instructor at four or five Maryland community colleges. I had my first interview at Baltimore Junior College but was told a few weeks later that I did not get the position. In April, I got a call asking me to interview for Anne Arundel Community College (AACC), three miles northwest of Annapolis. I went there and was interviewed by a professor who would later become my best friend and mentor, Dr. Enno Lohmann. He hired me on the spot, and during that difficult year of 1968. I had succeeded in obtaining a great position. I taught at AACC for forty-six years, until I retired in 2013.

However, I still had to finish my teaching at Annapolis High School and my last class at the University. And wouldn't you know it, another unusual incident occurred before the school year ended. Annapolis High had some traditions. One was the annual food fight that was started by the senior class in the school cafeteria. One never knew when it would happen. One year, a new vice principal, Mr. B., was determined to keep it from happening by coming into the cafeteria every day with a Polaroid camera. I will let you guess what happened when it did occur—just to say it was a messy situation for Mr. B. Fortunately for me, I was able to avoid the food fights because I never had cafeteria duty and hardly ever went to the cafeteria.

However, there was a tradition for psychology classes that started before I was hired. Each spring all psychology students had an opportunity to go on a field trip to the large psychiatric hospital, Crownsville State Hospital, near Annapolis. One day, a week before the trip, Tom Getz asked me if I would be willing to lead the trip in 1968 by myself. There was not very much to be gained but I had given my students the chance to go on the trip for the last three years. Now Tom was saying he just did not want to go. I should have picked up on the hidden message in our conversation, but I did not. It turned out he had twice as many students who wanted to go as I did. He had two buses of students. The only chaperones for the bus ride were two parents. I had one bus of students and agreed to be the only teacher to lead three buses of students on a field trip to a large psychiatric hospital.

We all arrived at the hospital, went through in groups and talked to some staff and psychiatric patients. Today, in the twenty first century, for many reasons this kind of field trip would be considered unnecessary and would not be allowed. In 1968 it was no big deal. After the trip was over, I thought everything went well.

The next day I got a memo that summoned me to Mr. Flack's office during my break. Later when I went to his office, he seemed a bit perturbed. "Mr. Shilkret," he said, "did you know that one of the students you took on the field trip, George Nock, passed out in his sixth-period English class?" This student was in Tom Getz's class, and I did not know him at all.

"No, sir," I replied.

"Well, he did. I want you to find out what happened and give me a full written report by the end of the week." I said I would and left his office.

You might wonder how I would find out what happened on a bus I was not on and in an English class I certainly was not in when George Nock passed out. I simply asked the students to tell me. I asked Tom Getz to send over some students who had been on the same bus as George to my classroom during our lunch break. They revealed everything that happened.

George Nock got on school bus number 3 with the other students, but he brought a bottle of wine. He began to drink the wine directly from the bottle as soon as the trip began. Then, after the short trip, he put the top on the bottle and left it covered in his jacket on the bus. He joined the other students as they went through the hospital. After the tour was over, he went back on bus number 3 and quickly started drinking more wine. When he finished the whole bottle, he threw the bottle out the window as the bus went back to the high school. All the buses got back to the high school in time for sixth period. George went to his English class and passed out in a few minutes after he entered. His teacher was dismayed and reported the incident to her principal. I delivered my report to Mr. Flack, and that was the end of my involvement. I did not speak to my principal about the incident but later heard that George Nock had been expelled from school.

The days went by fast in the spring of 1968, and right before June I met one of my friends, Jack Kelly, for a beer at Fred's, a local bar and restaurant. He told me an amusing story about the latest prank he had played on his students. It had been rumored for a week or so that Mr. Flack was going to retire. Jack said that a student asked him who would replace him as principal. Without hesitation Jack told his class that one of the teachers would replace Mr. Flack as principal. When another student asked how that would be decided Jack told them that the students would be able to vote for their principal in an election. The students believed him and got excited about the possibility of an election for principal. They even began asking their other teachers if they were going to run for principal. Jack could tell a convincing story!

Then I went over to AACC to talk to their dean of faculty about my salary for next year and to be formally hired as Instructor of psychology. He introduced himself, talked about the college for a few minutes, and then asked me what I was paid this year at the high school. I just said $8,500. He looked at me and said, "We can match that." I should have tried to suggest a higher salary, but I did not. I guess I was too excited about getting this new position.

Later in the week, I went into Mr. Flack's office to tell him of my plans for next year and how I had been hired by the community college. "Well, we will miss you, Mr. Shilkret," he said. I did not realize at the time how I would view my four years at Annapolis, or I would have spoken to him more.

That summer I spent days preparing for my classes at the college. But my mood was disturbed by the chaotic presidential election and the turmoil of the sixties. In June I stayed awake to watch the return of the California primary election on television. As I was watching the Kennedy victory party, I saw Robert Kennedy fall as he was walking through the crowd. He had been assassinated! I was shocked as I watched the events unfold. He had been my hero, and now he was gone. I felt horrible. It completely changed my summer, but I continued my preparations for my new job.

The first day I arrived at Anne Arundel Community College as a new instructor I realized how fortunate I was.

The professors I met were friendly and glad to meet me. I had been hired because of my background in developmental psychology and was looking forward to teaching it along with the introductory psychology course. I was given a private office. I would share a secretary with my new colleagues who would type all my tests and letters. There was a college print shop. I would never have to work a mimeograph machine again! I would also have some control over when I would teach my classes. Anne Arundel Community College was the only community college in the state where the faculty load was only four classes.

I taught psychology at Anne Arundel for forty-six years. I sometimes said that the best day was the first day of classes, and the second-best day was the last day of class. Actually, I went on and on, with summer classes, mid-semester two-week classes, extra classes at Bowie State and Catonsville Community College, and much later, online classes. I also said I was fortunate to only have one or two bad days at work a year

Jack 1967

Jack's yearbook photo

AUTHOR'S NOTE

I wrote this memoir in 2020 during the pandemic with the intention to have a record of my life when I was much younger in my twenties. I decided to be completely candid, so everything described in this book actually happened. I decided to use some false names because I did not want to embarrass anyone. I also forgot some names and made up names for that reason too.

Printed in the United States
by Baker & Taylor Publisher Services